ALCOCK
OF SALISBURY

Alcock of Salisbury.

First published privately in 1949.

Republished Travis & Emery 2009.

Published by
Travis & Emery Music Bookshop
17 Cecil Court, London, WC2N 4EZ, England.
Tel. (+44) 20 7240 2129.
neworders@travis-and-emery.com

ISBN Hardback: 978-1-906857-93-6   Paperback: 978-1-906857-94-3

"Alcock of Salisbury" was written and privately printed by Sir Walter's eldest daughter Judith (deceased).

This edition is produced with the kind permission of his surviving grandchildren.

ALCOCK
OF SALISBURY

Printed by
Derry & Sons, Limited,
Nottingham.
1949

" *Rest friend, no tears for you : much good befell
You living, and some ill—God's gift as well* ".

—H. Macnaughton, *from the Greek of Philetas.*

WALTER ALCOCK AT THE ORGAN OF SALISBURY CATHEDRAL IN HIS 84TH YEAR.

I

WALTER GALPIN ALCOCK was born on December 29th 1861 and died on September 11th 1947. He was born during the lifetime of Charles Dickens; he saw Wagner and Dvorak; he grew to manhood in a world without telephones or cars and in which broadcasting, at which he was to become an adept, had not been thought of. He lived under five sovereigns and assisted at the coronations of three of them. He saw science develop beyond the dreams of the scientists of his youth, accompanied by an unexampled acceleration of social change throughout the world. Though many men have lived as long, none can have brought to the procession of the years a livelier intelligence or a more sensitive alertness.

He came of a yeoman family of which records have been traced back continuously to the sixteenth century, an ordinary family, but one of which the members throughout the centuries showed a recurring persistence in rising above their circumstances and in taking their own line. It is interesting to observe in the genealogical account that has recently been made by Dr. Stanley Alcock of Reading how many of them had music in them. There was a John Alcock, a Mus. Doc., who was organist and composer at Lichfield Cathedral in the 18th century. There was another John Alcock born in 1855 who could play any musical instrument made and there was Arthur Alcock who was music master at Malvern College at the end of the last century who also illustrated the independence of the family genius by disappearing just before a school concert and enlisting for the South African war. Throughout the record the Alcocks are to be found playing this or that instrument, and a younger Walter Alcock, who runs a prosperous cattle business in New Zealand, emigrated there in 1927 with a violin under one arm and an attache case under the other as his only possessions.

This vigorous stock found its full flowering in Walter Galpin. He was the eldest of six children, all of whom showed an astonishing proficiency in anything they chose to give their minds to, but especially if it had to do with music. Frederick was a first class oboe player and after he retired from the Customs service succeeded in giving a good account of himself with both viola and 'cello. William was a fine tympanist, while Gilbert at the time of writing is still a church organist of high standing and a music master at Eastbourne College. Stanley, who composes anthems and masses and plays the organ, is also one of the best valuers of antiques in the country. The only girl, Florence, was the possessor of a pure and lovely soprano voice.

Their mother was Mary Galpin who married their father Walter William Alcock in 1860. Like many who are mothers of distinguished sons she was a woman of strong character and clear decision. When she died at the age of eighty her hair was as raven black as when she was a girl and her back as straight. She shared to the full the vitality of her husband's family. She had a precise and dignified way of speaking. As she grew older she produced an occasional spoonerism which would be treasured delightedly by her irreverent grandchildren, largely because of the stately way in which she delivered it, and she would laugh with them. Her best was achieved in speaking of a couple between whom a slight coolness had been noticed. " Depend upon it my dear " she said to her daughter, " There is a root in the lift " !

She was dearly loved by all her children and they owed much of their originality and unfettered development to her wise understanding. There were no repressions in that family in spite of a strict discipline.

When Walter was born his father was a village schoolmaster at Edenbridge in Sussex. His early days cannot have been in all respects easy. He was brought up in a stricter discipline than children know to day and his refusal to lay a hand in punishment on any child of his derived, as he told them, from his recollections of what he himself endured in those harsher days. Walter was a very nervous child, preferring often to be alone and content with some trifle to play with. Thunderstorms terrified him, as indeed they did all his life, not so much from fear of injury as from an instinctive dread of the power displayed, intensified, doubtless, by a physical effect on his highly strung nervous system.

In those Victorian days psychology played little part in a child's upbringing, but the nostalgia with which Walter Alcock looked back to his boyhood is proof that parental affection, such as he undoubtedly enjoyed, and the comfort of familiar things can cushion a child against many hard knocks. All his life, despite his delight in technical experiment, it was the old familiar things that he loved. It is not surprising that one of his generation should feel a nostalgia for the past.

The serenity and promise of the days of Alcock's youth seem to us now like a fairy-tale, but he and his contemporaries actually experienced that serenity and that promise. Alcock had, moreover, a retentive memory that etched for him indelible pictures on which he loved to gaze and his power of reliving the past was no doubt part of the secret of his eternal youth. Writing near the end of his life he told how as a boy of seven or eight he went with the schoolmistress of his village school whom he adored, to see hounds meet. " I connect her ", he writes, " with the beauty of the scene, and to this day a gorse bush with its yellow bloom and peculiar scent takes me back there and then I see her hair waving in the wind. Even primroses and violets, there to be found in profusion, have surely not retained the rare qualities of those enchanted days ".

When as a very small boy he was out walking with his father the two of them stepped back from the road to see

Charles Dickens drive by " with his ponies and his two lady passengers, the low-crowned hat of the period well over his eyes ". That picture was ever evoked for him by a convolvulus in the hedge, because he remembered how he had seen the flower then, growing beside the dusty road, with the great writer's head silhouetted against it.

In 1868 the family removed to Islington, Walter's father having obtained a post at The Middle Class School there, but in 1870 he was appointed first Superintendent of the Metropolitan and City Police Orphanage at Twickenham and this necessitated another removal. All this time Walter had little education as we know it today, which makes his facility for the spoken and written word all the more remarkable. But one has to remember that even the young lived much closer to culture then than they do today. The classical standard still obtained in any educated household and regular attendance at church and family prayers attuned their ears to the rhythm and harmonies of English at its finest. The country, with its ultimate values was still close to all. The wireless had not yet banished discussion and the restrictions of transport threw young and old upon their own resources. There is no doubt that Walter and his brothers were encouraged in their interests and hobbies by their parents from an early age and they had the stimulation that a large family gives.

A railway, for instance, always gripped Walter's imagination, even as a small child and when he was fourteen he constructed a model locomotive. The boiler consisted of a cocoa tin with its lid soldered on ; the frame was built up from strips of brass soldered together. He was unable to make a cylinder so he bought one. And he got the engine going. His father was so surprised that he gave the boy half-a-crown with which to buy another cylinder. He built the railway of wood and constructed points so that he could shunt the engine to another section. His tools included a soldering iron, a centre bit for drilling holes with the sharp end of a file and his mother's best scissors.

But music claimed first interest in the Alcock family circle. Walter's father was an amateur 'cellist and the possessor of a beautiful baritone voice. His influence on his son's musical education was of great value, though his ambition that he should specialise as a pianist was defeated by the boy's passion for the organ. Walter was soon able to play simple accompaniments for his father and, though such works were far beyond his capacity at the time, they struggled through Beethoven's A Major Cello Sonata and the two sonatas by Mendelssohn, while they actually worked at trios by Beethoven, Mendelssohn, Mozart and Reisseger, though often without a violin. And Walter tells how he was occasionally hauled out of bed to play accompaniments when friends dropped in for music.

By the time he was twelve, Walter was acting as deputy organist to Mr. Sugg, organist of St. Mary's, Twickenham, whose organ pupil he had become. But his first real step towards his great career was made possible by Lady Freake of Fulwell Park. Her husband, Sir Charles Freake, presented the building for the new National Training School for Music which in 1883 became the temporary home of the Royal College of Music and is now familiar as the headquarters of the Royal College of Organists. In 1875 Walter Alcock, nominated by Lady Freake as a candidate, obtained a scholarship, tenable for five years and became one of the first students.

One pictures him, a slim, simplehearted boy of fourteen, untouched by life, full of wonder and expectation, making the daily journey from Twickenham to Kensington, via

Addison Road, in company with his friend E. T. Sweeting. His masters were those whose names have become part of the tradition of English music—Sullivan, Stainer, Bridge, Monk. Stainer it was who invited him to sit with him in the organ loft at St. Paul's Cathedral and that was Alcock's introduction to the work of the great " Father " Willis, the organ builder whose firm was responsible for the superb instrument at Salisbury that was to become Alcock's care and joy in the years to come. All his life he remembered and gave thanks for the standards of musicianship and worship that Stainer showed him in those days.

II

IN 1880, at the age of nineteen, Alcock was appointed organist of St. Mary's, Twickenham, in succession to Mr. Sugg who had been his first teacher of the organ. His parents had lately moved to Somerset so that he was now living alone with, at first, very little money and little apparent chance of advancement. His youth and inexperience were, indeed, hardly likely to attract pupils. The few years following the end of his musical education were hard times for him, for he was entirely dependent on himself, with a very small stipend from the church and very little knowledge of the world. But the charm which characterised him throughout his long life soon won him a number of friends who gave him practical help when he most needed it, finding him pupils, making it possible for him to meet many distinguished people and constantly enlarging his acquaintance among those of influence.

Alcock's principal recreation at this time was cycling. An overmastering love of the open road, combined with his inate interest in engines and the problems of mechanical propulsion made of him a predestined cyclist and, later, motorist. From his boyhood in the early seventies when his enthusiasm was first kindled, until the end of his life when he was still driving his Austin Ten himself, he was lost unless he knew that in shed or garage lay that " something on wheels " which to him spelt freedom. He was the supreme joy-rider.

The spark was first lit on the day in early youth when he saw a man riding a contraption that ran on three wheels; the leading wheel was 26 in. in diameter and to it was attached a bathchair steering handle. The wheel on the left was 36 in., the driving wheel 50 in. The latter was actuated by pedals driving a knife-grinder crank.

Walter dreamed of this engine and of the glad day when he might come to possess such an one himself. At last he contrived to buy one secondhand. This cherished possession eventually betrayed the enthusiasm lavished on it. Its doom was sealed after its performance on a journey planned to convey its rider from Twickenham to Somerset. With a friend who was riding a 55 in. high bicycle, Walter set forth at 5 a.m. It began to rain and it rained all day.

The roads were of course deep in mud and the solid tyres took it in turns to leave the rims to which they had then to be reattached by means of string. The travellers ploughed across Hartford Bridge Flats against a strong wind and eventually reached Basingstoke (37 miles) after twelve hours on the road !

Soon after this adventure a trusting friend lent Alcock a 52 in. bicycle, the model known as the pennyfarthing. After practising on a lawn he took the machine out and rode down past Twickenham Green, narrowly missing collision with the Virgina Water coach on the way. His conversion was immediate and complete and having sold his three-wheeler he acquired a high bicycle. He soon became an expert rider. All his life he was a joy to watch on a bicycle, his wheel steady, his pedalling rhythmic, his machine under perfect control.

No later machine, not even the motor car, ever enthralled him as did the bicycle of those early days. And indeed it must have been a most delightful form of progression on quiet country roads, gravelled and smooth, meeting only an occasional farm cart or other cyclist, lifted high above the hedges so that the countryside rolled spacious to the view on all sides. All through the years some scent or fleeting thought would recall for Alcock the flavour of that enchanted time and the roads of Hampshire and Dorset enshrined for him his most nostalgic memories.

Twickenham had, of course, its Bicycle Club. Alcock joined it in 1881 and later became its Captain. " What an unmitigated nuisance we bicyclists must have been in those far-off days," he wrote. " We were very precise in our costume which consisted of breeches and tunic, lined with flannel and close fitting. A polo cap completed the rig-out. The Captain carried a bugle, which he blew on the Club's approach to village or town. We used to ride forth, perhaps twenty or thirty strong, claiming the road as our exclusive property.

" We took part in the annual Hampton Court Meet, at which Clubs from all parts mustered on Hampton Court Green. On the signal being given we set off through Hampton, Teddington, Bushey Park and round the Diana Fountain to the Green once more, where the riders dismounted and the show was over. How thrilling it was for me when I as Captain led my Club through the gates of Hampton Court to cries of ' Well ridden Twickenham ' ! "

The mounting of the high bicycle with as few hops as possible was one of the ideals of the cyclist of those days, Alcock was eventually able to reach the saddle with one hop and was correspondingly proud. On descending a hill the correct thing to do was to put the legs over the handlebars. This looked very dangerous, but it was safer than pedalling when, in case of a fall, you came down on your head, whereas if your legs were over the handlebars you alighted on your feet. Young Alcock used to enjoy performing this trick in the street, thereby occasioning much concern among solicitous passers-by, who thought he had done it by accident.

He once rode from Southampton to Twickenham without leaving the saddle, why, he said, he had no idea, though perhaps it was because the journey *to* Southampton had been of a very different nature. Owing to a strong head wind which grew ever stronger, he became so exhausted that on the outskirts of Guildford he threw himself on a bank and literally cried with fatigue, but struggled on to the top of the Hog's Back where the wind in that exposed place made riding an impossibility and he was glad to accept a lift from a farm cart that was returning to Farnham from Guildford market. As he sat there he noticed that the rear fork of his bicycle was cracked—it was a 50 in. racer and too light for road work. From Farnham therefore, he returned to Surbiton by train to collect his roadster, which a friend had borrowed, and set out once more for Farnham where he spent the night and continued his way to Beaulieu the next day. There could be no doubt about his enthusiasm for cycling!

Some time during the eighties the safety bicycle made its appearance and Alcock adopted in turn most of its many and various forms that gradually resolved themselves into the type we know today. Great was the enthusiasm over the inventions of those early days and many the aids to better cycling. When Alcock invested in a pair of pedals with ball-bearings he would have been furious had anyone told him that they made little difference to his speed. In later years he used to look with much amusement at the Cycling section in old numbers of the Badminton series, that recalled to him so vividly the experiences of that simple epoch. He and one of his brothers used often to talk in those days of the possibility of attaching an engine of some kind to their cycles, so that they might more easily mount the hills or ride against the wind. How little they guessed what the realisation of that fancy was to do to their world!

III

ALCOCK was engaged as a proof-reader by Novello & Co. in 1885, but he soon found that with his Church work this left him too little leisure and he had also begun to compose in a small way. He therefore left Novello's after a year. He was still true to his ambition to become a cathedral organist. Finding that there was no chance at all for him at St. Paul's, where he would so dearly have loved to work under Stainer, he went to Dr. Frederick Bridge at the Abbey and became one of his assistants. This eventually led to his becoming the first Assistant Organist of the Abbey to be appointed by the Dean and Chapter—a post he held for thirty years. At about the same date he also received the appointment of organist to Quebec Chapel, now the Church of the Annunciation in Bryanston Street. Although this was promotion he must have been sorry to leave Twickenham. There he had found his first post, there he had been Captain of his Bicycle Club. The foundations of his knowledge of the steam locomotive were laid at Twickenham, where he made many friends among the drivers in the engine sheds there and in those spacious days was allowed to ride with them on the footplates of their engines and occasionally to drive them. He once pulled up the Bournemouth express at Waterloo and never forgot it.

It was in 1892, when Alcock was thirty-one, that he met Naomi Blanche Lucas of Preston, Rutland. It was entirely by chance. She was an amateur violinist and at some musical At Home where she was to play, her accompanist failed her and her hostess found Walter to take his place. Naomi Lucas was a very lovely woman in the days when there were few aids to loveliness. Walter evidently lost no time in acquainting her with his interests.

" My dear ", said Miss Lucas to her sister, " I have met the most extraordinary man. He plays the piano divinely and he drives an engine ! "

Walter Alcock proved to have other attractions also and on a day in January, 1893, they were married in the village church at Preston. The coachman who drove them in a brougham to the station six miles away still lives in that village and still talks of how it rained that day.

The marriage was to prove a most devoted partnership of fifty-four years. During all that time husband and wife were never parted for so much as a day without writing to one another. It is hard to concieve what Alcock's life might have been if he had found a wife less loving, less understanding, less ready to identify her interests with his. In his later years he mellowed in every way, but it cannot have been an easy start for the pair. Not only was there very little money to support their establishment of two rooms in Bryanston Street, but husband and wife came from totally different backgrounds. He had grown up in a suburb of London with little education but his music and no knowledge of any interests outside his own. She was the daughter of parents whose families had owned their estates for generations and who took for granted a culture and breeding of which he knew nothing. That the adjustment was made is proof, not only of their deep affection, but of a higher code of discipline and sacrifice than is usually accepted today. It was fortunate for Alcock that this was so. From the beginning his home was the fulcrum of his life. Despite money worries, (occasionally desperate) intense pressure of work and a large and very young family (there were five of them under four, including

twins, by January 1898) his house was always to him the
" still centre " of rest. His love for it was the outstanding
fact in his life. He never willingly spent a night away from
it and when, as an examiner for the Associated Board, he
had to leave it for a week or more, he was clouded with
depression for days beforehand and returned like a boy
released from school.

In 1894 Alcock deputised as organist at Salisbury for
three months, a significant event, for from then on that
" silent finger " beckoned him to the eventual fulfilment
of his early dreams.

In the following year he was appointed organist at Holy
Trinity, Sloane Street, where under the sympathetic and
benevolent authority of his Rector, Archdeacon Bevan, he
was able to develop to the full his powers as an organist,
as a church musician and as a choir trainer.

His time was now very well filled as he had four days a
week at the Abbey in addition to the daily service and choir
practice at Holy Trinity. Pupils came along in ever
increasing numbers, he was appointed a professor at the
Royal College of Music and he was becoming wellknown
as a recitalist.

In 1900 he moved with his wife and family of six girls to Kingston-on-Thames, whence he caught the 8.21 train to Waterloo every morning, Sundays included. He never regretted the change and his love of the road found a new outlet in driving a series of experimental motor vehicles into the surrounding country during his leisure hours. It was a busy, satisfying life, his work congenial and done amongst congenial people, with the consciousness that he had made good in his chosen profession in spite of many handicaps, his wife and children round him, his hobbies and amusements absorbing and interesting. He was so content that when in 1902 he was offered the post of organist to His Majesty's Chapels Royal he was on the point of refusing it. His more worldly-wise friends, however, among whom was Sir John Stainer, warned him that even at some sacrifice of artistic fulfilment it was an honour that must be accepted, involving as it did work of high significance. He left Holy Trinity with the greatest regret and it is probably true to say that he was happier there than in any other post he ever held.

His Sundays after this appointment became very strenuous indeed. He would play for Matins at St. James'

Palace, Marlborough House and, when the King was in London, at Buckingham Palace as well. His duties as Assistant Organist at Westminster made him responsible for the afternoon service at the Abbey and he would then go back to St. James' Palace for evensong. No wonder that when he reappeared at 8.0 p.m. or after among his family the children learnt to be quiet and no musical instrument might be played. And woe betide the girl who was heard whistling—a form of self-expression that, tired or not, Alcock always considered belonged to musical morons. But though the work was hard and sometimes ungrateful the position was one of great prestige and interest. It was through this appointment that Alcock played at the coronations of Edward VII and George V and though, by then no longer in Royal service, was invited, in deference to his high position in the world of Church music to do so again at the coronation of George VI. He felt, however, that on this occasion a younger man should be given his opportunity, but he undertook all the necessary improvisation and he accompanied Parry's anthem " I Was Glad " sung at the entrance of the King, as at the two previous coronations. It was as he entered the Abbey on this third occasion that he replied " Season " ! to the official enquiry for his ticket of admittance—a quirk of humour entirely characteristic of him and of his calm, however awe-inspiring the circumstances.

By the end of the first decade of this century Walter Alcock was recognised as amongst the foremost of his country's organists and up to 1916 he was a busy London musician holding important organ posts, a distinguished member of the staff of the Royal College, an examiner for the Associated Board, besides building up a great reputation as a recitalist. But just as his career seemed to be reaching its climax he suddenly gave up nearly all his London work to become organist of Salisbury Cathedral. It is evident from the musical press of that date that his decision was inexplicable to most of his colleagues, but to him it was the fulfilment of a dream, and though he met disillusionment as we all must who grasp our dreams, it is certain he never regretted that sudden decision to leave the clamour and rewards of London for the green close of Salisbury.

There he lived for the rest of his life, still playing the great organs up and down the country, travelling to London to see his friends and to teach at the Royal College, training generation after generation of choristers to sing with the

The Organist's House in Salisbury Close.

Driving his Great Northern Model
at the Age of 75.

Walter (*left*) and his Brother William
with their Tandem Bicycle 1890.

With Simon.

His First Motor Car.
A 6 H.P. Rover about 1905.

purity and fullness of tone that has become a hallmark of Salisbury. Quiet evensongs, the Church's festivals, great occasions—all found him there with the magnificent Willis instrument he adored, tended, tuned with his own hands and restored, that seemed to speak for him as for no other as a thoroughbred will always respond to the master.

IV

WHEN Alcock was knighted in 1933 he received some three hundred letters, while a procession of telegraph boys brought a hundred telegrams from all over the world. It was a far cry from the lonely struggling days at Twickenham. He himself seemed bewildered by the volume of congratulations. There was very genuine rejoicing at the recognition accorded him and it was due as much to love of the man as to admiration for his achievements. In his long life Alcock won and held the affection of many outstanding personalities. He possessed a faculty for uncritical loyalty which was very endearing and his genuine admiration for the achievements of others was naturally enhanced where his friends were concerned. With some, among them E. T. Sweeting, who before he went as music master to Rossall and Winchester, shared Alcock's early days at the National Training College there was the nostalgic pull of the past. Charles Macpherson who followed Sir George Martin as organist of St. Paul's was perhaps Alcock's closest and most loved friend. He was not an easy man to know—he was silent and far too modest. To his intimate friend, however, his fund of pawky humour, his fine musicianship and his penetrating thought made him the most charming of companions. They used to sit at the same piano and extemporise duets together in a way that had they chosen to commercialize it would have made organ playing for a livelihood unnecessary for them, but to them it was just a pastime. Macpherson's death at a comparatively early age was a loss for which nothing could compensate his friend.

There were many who, though not professional musicians, had a sincere love of music that brought them in contact with Alcock and it was interesting to see how often a genuine and lasting friendship would spring up between this remarkable man and those whose lives had fallen in very different places and with whom he might not have been expected to have much in common. For though music was often the cause of their meeting it did not form the basis of the friendship's continuance. Alcock, like many professional musicians, took no particular pleasure in discussing the job when off duty. Yet, though he was not an educated man, in the sense that he had never been to school, he was a most welcome guest, for instance, among the Lubbocks, that brilliant cultured family, whom he first met when he was at Holy Trinity and how he loved to stay with them at Emmetts, near Sevenoaks, talking of motor cars and astronomy and luxuriating in a spacious comfort of which his early years had taught him nothing.

While Alcock was at Holy Trinity a sporting Squire, one Meredith Brown, with a quirk for music, applied to him for organ lessons. He played terribly badly with little hope of improvement and his lessons generally ended at his request as a private organ recital by Alcock. They became devoted friends, though Meredith Brown was by many years the senior. He used to ask Alcock to his beautiful place near Chippenham and his admiration for him was such that he would not believe that he did not do everything as well as he played the organ. He did, in fact, find him a very apt pupil with the shot gun, but a day came when he decided that he should have a day's hunting. Deaf to Alcock's protests that he had never been on a horse in his life, he made him put on full hunting regalia, and with the aid of an amused but apprehensive groom Alcock found himself astride a seventeen hand hunter that was full of corn and happy anticipation. They moved off in the direction of the meet but the nearer they got to it the nearer Alcock got to the horse's neck and his host finally barked out : " You'd better go back. You're no good at this sort of thing ". " I told you I wasn't " said Alcock and was led home. He said that Meredith Brown never quite forgave him for failing to live up to his illusions about him !

The Reginald McKennas at Mells, Mr. Sadler at Weacombe in the Quantocks, Henry Moffat in the New Forest, Lord and Lady Malise Graham, the Devenishes at Durnford, the Booth Joneses at Hale Park—they and many others made him free of their houses where the quiet and beauty on all sides were a never-failing joy and wonder to him. His enjoyment of everything, his fund of anecdotes, his quick wit, made him a very welcome guest and it is to be hoped that those who gave him such unfailing kindness and friendship may realise what a contribution they made to his life.

Among those of his own profession, of course, his friendships covered a wide arc. Sir John Stainer, though older by many years, was a source of the greatest inspiration to him and was a very good friend indeed when in his early years he needed both guidance and encouragement. He had the highest opinion of Stainer as a Church musician and felt that those who condemned him on account of his compositions knew only half the story, for he was a genius at improvisation and there is no doubt that it was in listening to him that Alcock began to develop that same gift in himself which reached such great heights. When Sir George Martin followed Stainer at St. Paul's Alcock was already becoming known as an organist and it was then that he entered into the company of those who at the turn of the century were the giants in the world of Church music. Sir Walter Parratt, organist at St. George's, Windsor and Master of the King's Music, Sir Hubert Parry Director of the Royal College of Music, Sir Charles Stanford, the eminent composer, were all writing and teaching alongside him. They were among his lifelong friends and what an unbounded affection he had for them, especially for Parratt, who was a man of vastly greater mental equipment than himself. Alcock considered him one of the greatest teachers of the organ, as indeed he was, and was aware that Parratt had that hallmark of the born teacher in that he could always bring what he wanted to say within the comprehension of the dullest. Alcock himself, though notable for the success of his pupils in examinations, did not find it easy to cope with those of slow perception and he has described how when he was in Parratt's room during the giving of a lesson the pupil was content to play a pedal E which should have been E flat. " Oh Sir ", said Parratt " E Flat, E Flat ". But the E natural went booming on until Parratt reduced it all to its simplest terms. " Sir ", he said, " You have your boot on the wrong piece of wood ". This was the kind of thing that delighted Alcock and he was fascinated too by Parratt's " brain-teasers ", telling of how he used to play one or other of Handel's classical pieces while calling out the moves of two games of chess. " I saw him ", he wrote " play a Bach Trio in which he used the 12th for the right-hand part. This involved transposing that part a 12th lower—a process which apparently gave him immense pleasure ". It did not occur to him that Parratt probably viewed his manipulations of a car's inner parts with equal wonder.

In the *Graphic* for June 24th, 1911 appeared a row of six portraits, those of the modern composers of the music for the coronation of George V. These were Sir Charles Stanford, Sir Walter Parratt, Sir Edward Elgar, Sir John

Stainer and Alcock—an apt illustration of the position the last-named had by then achieved in the musical world. The portraits were superimposed on a musical stave, the key indicated being that of G flat, with its signature of 6 flats. Alcock saw the hand of Sir Frederick Bridge in this and accusing him of the jibe suggested that an enharmonic change to F sharp with its signature of six sharps would have been more appropriate. The episode is typical of the two men. While Alcock was incomparably the more brilliant he nevertheless appreciated to the full Bridge's experience and sense of showmanship and a steady affection born of thirty years workaday companionship existed between them.

When Sir Hugh Allen became Director of the Royal College of Music he and Alcock had not known each other very well and for a time the two men were for some reason slightly at odds. Sir Hugh had a bluff and downright manner and was in the habit of scoring off all and sundry as occasion offered. It was not long before Alcock's quick wit proved more than a match for him and that disarming personality did the rest. They became close friends and Allen did as much as anyone to see that Alcock's services to the world of music received their due recognition. In the Professors' dining room at the Royal College the two would sit side by side exchanging stories and wisecracks and their end of the table was always a focus of laughter. Musicians are on the whole a lighthearted race and Alcock was in his element here. When travelling during the War became too great a strain for him and he had to resign from the Royal College it was for him the beginning of the end. He never ceased to miss the congenial companionship that he had known for nearly fifty years.

Among the men of his own generation were Henry Ley of Eton, Bairstow of York, Harold Darke and Walford Davies. There existed between him and such men the affection born of a community of interests and a deep sense of each others worth. In Walford Davies especially, Alcock found an ever-kindly adviser on his compositions, encouraging, astringent and constructive.

But the presiding genius of Alcock's musical life was Elgar, whose great works crystallized for him all that he demanded from music. There was something mystical in his conception of him as a composer and he listened to his works, not indeed with any lessening of the critical faculty, but with a sense of fulfilment which no other composer could give him. Characteristically, by a natural transference Elgar was to him the most admirable of men and though they were never intimate their friendship was to Alcock one of the most valued experiences of his life. The signed copy of " The Dream of Gerontius " which Elgar gave him was among his most treasured possessions.

His feeling for Elgar was indeed the concentrate of Alcock's genius for friendship. His admiration for those he loved was unquestioning and it never seemed to occur to him that those of whom he thought so highly had an equal object of admiration in himself. Vaughan Williams arrived unexpectedly in Salisbury once, exhausted and at a loss for inspiration. He asked Alcock to play to him in the Cathedral after it was closed and Alcock played for two hours and was genuinely surprised at the gratitude and admiration of his old pupil, who went away refreshed and restored. Many of his friends must look back with happiness to a similar experience—the Cathedral, vast, brooding in darkness, the gleam from the console light and Alcock at the organ.

V

ALCOCK was a man of exceptional abilities and he might well have made his mark in any profession. He was in fact offered the choice by his father of entering either engineering or music and it is interesting to speculate what would have been the result had he chosen the former. But he did not hesitate; for as long as he could remember he had wanted to play the organ. When quite small he would sit at a writing desk pulling out the drawers as stops while one of his brothers pretended to blow. His one ambition was to become a cathedral organist and though nearly half a century was to elapse before he realised the burning desire of his boyhood he ranked then among the giants of his chosen profession. He himself in the later years of his life would deprecate his own technical abilities. He considered himself outstripped by such brilliant executants as George Cunningham or Thalben Ball, yet his playing was such that though there is no such thing as " touch " in the pianistic sense on the organ, it was possible to tell when he took over from another even in the middle of a hymn. " He has mastered the king of instruments and made it his servant ", said Sir Hubert Parry of Alcock and that mastery was of the essence of his performance. No doubt much of the brilliance of his technique came to him as part of his great natural gift—there was for him not much difficulty and he never found the struggles of beginners and amateurs easy to understand. He may have been right in thinking that the more modern exponents had outstripped him in technical performance but to very few is there given as to him such a sense of fitness, such unerring taste. He used to say he was always sorry when the Psalms were over, yet he played them twice a day for the greater part of his life. Therein lies perhaps the secret of the way he used to play them. His alert imagination was ever stirred by those majestic words and his response never failed, but always the organ was the partner, not the leader of the choir, as indeed in all his playing of the services. Aspiring organists who make the anthems and canticles a vehicle for an organ recital might have learnt more than technique from him.

He was an acknowledged master of improvisation and here his imagination and sense of fitness were exemplified at their best. As a young man he often included extemporisations in his recital programmes and these were of course fully developed and were of a very high standard of excellence. He considered that the ability to improvise was an important part of any organist's equipment and he was an outstanding example of the contribution it can make to a church service, even when used only as what has been aptly described as " musical matting " to cover the footfalls of a procession. He used to say, " Even if that may not be a high incentive to one's inspiration there is no reason why the contribution need be inartistic ".

His use there of the word contribution is the key to the faultless taste his work as a church musician invariably showed, from those quiet ingoing voluntaries at Salisbury to his triumphant improvisations at the last coronation. Of the latter he said, " I fear I made a great deal of noise and this occurred to me more than once while playing. I tried the effect of softening down, only to realise that after all a pean of triumph was what was called for ". That was his touchstone—that sense of the occasion which, while largely instinctive was enhanced by the sensitive imagination of an artist in complete control of his medium. No one who ever heard him at the organ during a wedding service will readily forgive the jerky, noisy selections so often offered as a background for what is after all a sacrament of the Church.

Alcock possessed in full measure that power of quick action, of anticipation, that is essential to any musician who performs in concert with others, most especially to an organist. He used to tell a story of King Edward VII's coronation. There was then no system of telephones and through a misunderstanding Parry's anthem, " I Was Glad " was sung right through before the King had arrived. There was a moment's pause and then Sir Frederick Bridge, who was conducting on a platform over Alcock's head called down, " Play for all you're worth ". So Alcock improvised for what to him seemed like an eternity, but was in fact twenty-six minutes and he had to be ready at any moment to move into the anthem again as soon as he received the signal. More than thirty years later he was improvising an introduction to that same anthem at George VI's coronation. As he played Dr. Bullock called to him : " Alcock, fifteen seconds more and finish in B flat ". Alcock's own comment on these incidents shows a happy fusing of two of his great enthusiasms and is entirely characteristic.

" It is at such moments that modulation from key to key must be under control. So many long accepted rules are disregarded today and to speak of the Neapolitan 6th, the Augmented 7th or the Dominant 7th raises a pitying smile on the faces of the younger guard. But I find it useful to employ such chords at will, any one of which might be called a Clapham Junction chord. It is possible to travel to almost any key by their means. As I went on I could not know when I might have to stop and as my final chord must have some relation to the coming fanfare from the State Trumpeters it was essential I should arrive punctually and on the right line. Once there I ran into the key of B flat, applying the brake so as to join up with the trumpets which introduced the anthem at the entry of the Queen ".

He was seventy-five on that last occasion. It was typical of his unruffled calm under any circumstances when he was performing. Not that he did not know all the nervous excitement that any great artist must experience when about to face an audience, but always his technique and experience triumphed, together with that sense of proportion which was the mainspring of his humour. This was particularly true when he was broadcasting. The few moments before the start were always a trial to his nerves and the balance tests which sometimes necessitated his presence on the organ stool a full hour before his time of playing must have been a severe strain physically as well as nervously for he was well over sixty when he began to broadcast. Add to this that he had to remember the selected combination of stops to be used and to keep within his scheduled time. But he appeared quite calm, quite deliberate, and he would often make jokes to anyone sitting beside him as occasion offered.

He played his first church service when he was eleven and his last when he was eighty-five. Never once did his interest and enjoyment flag. He found some things irksome —he did not enjoy teaching and he found conducting, except of special well-loved works, very uncongenial. He found the application necessary to composing alien to his nature, so that he produced far less than he might have done. But never in all his long life was he heard to repine at the prospect of playing even the simplest service. He used to say that while playing at one service he found himself looking forward to the next.

His enjoyment in the handling of organs remained with him all his life. He found it a thrilling experience to play on the Walker organ at York Minster at its opening in 1903 and his contribution to the opening series of recitals on the immense organ in Liverpool Cathedral was an equal joy to him. He displayed to the full on that occasion his astoundingly quick grasp of an organ's lay-out. He was able to get only three hours' practice and though anxious and nervous beforehand, on going to the console for the recital he felt perfectly happy and listened to his own playing with complete detachment, carried away by the effect of the splendid instrument, its imposing surroundings and the significance of the occasion.

" The complexity of the instrument troubled me not at all ", he wrote, " for it was all so admirably arranged. That day remains one of my most pleasant memories ".

No organ presented any real complexity to him, nor did the smallest instrument fail to respond to his inspired touch. He could bring all heaven about him through a two manual organ in a village church. They say animals can recognise those who love them. There seemed to be the same sense of recognition as the organs spoke for Alcock. It was of course his innate love of the instrument interpreted by his surpassing skill. During the last week in which he was able to reach the Salisbury organ-loft before his doctor told him that he must give up his work, his daughter who helped him there each day used to fear he would collapse on ascending the staircase, so feeble and exhausted had he become. But the moment he found himself on the organ it was as though new life flowed into him. His voice strengthened, he inspected the music and prepared the instrument and his playing was still as of old.

Alcock spoke very little of his own performances and never asserted his theories. It was as though he felt that the truths of good organ playing must be self-evident. But he had very definite views on the fundamentals of performance. He used to say he always found it easier to give recitals on large organs in spacious buildings than on smaller instruments in the ordinary church or hall. "The latter offer no help from their acoustical properties while you must be note perfect and sure of your registration. That is, of course, the ideal wherever you play but there can be no doubt that a reverberating building may help you at some awkward corner. A vital rule is to exercise control over rhythm and allow no mechanical appliances to affect it. Accuracy in time details is preferable to minute accuracy of notes at the expense of rhythm. As to speed, it is disquieting to observe the almost universal disregard of what is suitable. Many of our fine players appear to be more anxious to parade their fluency than to interpret what they are playing. Though opinions may vary as to the pace, say, of a Bach Fugue, such music does suggest dignity and this modern slick playing is inimical to that dignity and also alien to the instrument ".

Such was Alcock's creed. Of him on his death Dr. Thomas Armstrong wrote :

" He had been a pupil of Sullivan and Stainer. A man who was seventy when Alcock was born would have been alive with Hayden and Mozart. When you heard him play you recognised the significance of these facts, for his performances had a sense of style and a serene classical perfection that were unmistakable. What brilliance there was in his passage work ! What fire in his handling of a Bach Toccata ! What restraint and climax in his fugue playing ! It was virile, impassioned, romantic but controlled. No academic pretension here about making it sound like some emasculated eighteenth century instrument ! And at eighty Alcock was all that he had been at fifty, with an added mellowness. It was wonderful ! "

VI

BESIDES being a skilled performer Alcock was a highly efficient organist. The two do not necessarily go together. To him the organ was primarily an instrument to be used in the worship of God and there is no doubt that his apprenticeship under such men as Stainer and his contemporaries influenced him throughout his life. In the first thirty years, too, of his work religious feeling and reverence for the services of the church were taken for granted. Alcock was no theologian, his beliefs were extremely simple and his churchmanship of the plainest. He had a deep-rooted objection to ritualism and he was suspicious of all forms of " high " churchmanship. When in Salisbury Cathedral the practice was adopted whereby the priest retained the Chalice in his own hands at the Administration, Alcock was so outraged that he refused to attend another celebration in the Cathedral. The authorities, one is glad to remember, on hearing of this assured him the practice should not be extended to him and he returned. But he had a deep sense of worship which pervaded all his work and though he used to tell stories of his lapses of taste in his early years there is no doubt that he was extremely sensitive to atmosphere and his reaction to any occasion was, as has been seen, instinctively right.

He felt strongly that an organist carried great responsibility. " In his hands ", he said, " lies the power of aiding or hindering the devout worship of the congregation. The ministry of the church organist is essentially a spiritual ministry and as such ranks next to that of the clergy ".

This was his unshakable belief, but others had to be convinced and his main struggle was often, to his own everlasting amazement, with the clergy. He was astounded by the fact that leading members of the Church, holding high ecclesiastical office, should suggest such lamentable lack of education by their abysmal ignorance on matters of music and its place in the services for which they were responsible. That there could exist men in charge of souls to whom the value of this art in the service of God had not occurred was to him extraordinary. He urged unceasingly the importance of a proper relationship between an organist and his Rector or Vicar and had a fund of anecdotes to illustrate what was to him a disastrous lack of understanding between the two offices, a lack which he himself had once or twice experienced, though in the main he was, as might have been expected, fortunate in this respect. Archdeacon Bevan, who was Rector of Holy Trinity, Sloane Street when Alcock was organist was a man of great musical culture and appreciation. He recognised his young organist's gifts and under his sympathetic and encouraging stimulus Alcock brought the music of the services there to a high distinction. Several members of the choir, Walter Hyde among them, graduated to the concert platform and the opera and the " great days " are still remembered there. When Alcock was appointed at Salisbury in 1917 Archdeacon Carpenter was Precentor. For years the two worked in a harmony that was the natural result of deep mutual appreciation. Carpenter, like Bevan, knew that the Cathedral had in Alcock a devoted servant and a man of true greatness in his own sphere. Dean Randolph of Salisbury too, was one of whom Alcock spoke again and again, telling of his unfailing friendship, encouragement and guidance.

He had known, however of many organists who were not so fortunate. He used to tell of an advertisement he saw for an organist in which the vicar desired one who would for a stipend of £20 a year, play the services, do work in the vicar's garden and drive a small Singer. " I know ", said Alcock, " that we organists are prone to drive our small singers, but why the garden ? "

He himself was invited by a clergyman to open an organ that had just been installed " and when I mentioned a fee he replied that he thought I should enjoy a day in the country, but that he could not pay a fee. I felt it my duty to inform him that I made my living by such work and I heard no more ".

A young vicar who was completely unmusical told Alcock that his organist had objected to a certain hymn-tune on the ground that he considered it musically unworthy. The vicar went on : " I insisted on having it for if you give in to your organist you are done ".

The attitude of mind such stories show was to Alcock incomprehensible. Why, he would ask, employ and pay an expert and then refuse to allow that his opinion be worth having ? Where the musical services of the church are concerned there must, he knew, be partnership between the two or the results must fall short of the best. Uninformed criticism is to be found everywhere, but the way of the expert is hard when it comes from his superior officer.

Alcock felt strongly that a great deal was amiss with the status of the church organist in this country and he was always ready to take up the cudgels. The main ground of his complaint was that the low salaries and poor conditions of work presupposed a complete lack of appreciation of an organist's functions.

" It should be recognised ", he said in 1919, addressing the Salisbury Diocesan Association of Organists, " that an organist receives his appointment for Church work and not as a teacher of music. He takes office on the understanding that his Church work is to be his first consideration. But in how many churches is this claim justified by the salary paid ? For years past the church organist has had to live on a starvation wage and has often been compelled to work twelve hours a day in order to get enough teaching to keep body and soul together ".

Alcock knew what he was talking about. He had had to do it himself. But if he crusaded on behalf of his brothers in the profession he set high standards for them. He deplored any tendency on the part of the organist to intrude on his hearers and his own conduct of the daily services was a model of restraint and good taste, though that he knew how to use the full range of any instrument was patent to all who heard his outgoing voluntaries on triumphant occasions or his accompaniments of festal services. He was continually warning organists against becoming too secular, against becoming " showy and meretricious seekers after notoriety and self-advancement ". While he was ever jealous for his art and her place in the worship of the Church he never claimed any recognition for himself and was genuinely astonished all his life when people, some of them of great distinction, praised his work.

" We need not apologise for our instrument ", he once said. " Is it not a worthy exponent of lofty thought and suggestion ? " But he felt there was a danger lest organists, provided with instruments of increasing size and scope, should forget what they were really there for.

" We organists ", he wrote, " are far from blameless. For too long have we allowed our enthusiasm for our instrument to blind us to its true mission, whilst neglecting study of the liturgical side of our work. Far more care in suitable accompaniment is needed, while unaccompanied singing should be still further encouraged. We must remember too, that the music is not the chief consideration and that its function is but an added appeal. The organ of today is, no doubt through the tendency among organists to develop their powers as recitalists, often larger than is actually necessary for the general purposes of accompaniment. But the greater includes the less and stops may be found suitable to all requirements, whatever the size of the instrument ".

The standards he set for performance he applied also to music to be performed. He loathed the cheap and sentimental, feeling such things to be sacrilege. Many hymn tunes were a sore trial to him and even at their best he felt them to be of little musical import. No " old association " will reconcile any artist to what he knows is aesthetically worthless and Alcock often wondered why meretricious music should be admitted where false doctrine was abhorred. Yet even here his sense of the needs of worshippers modified his disapproval.

"However good a hymn or its tune may be the combination can seldom be satisfactory as only in rare cases can the tune suit every verse. Multitudes of examples may be seen by a cursory glance at any hymnbook. The undoubted fact remains, however, that the poorest hymns may, by tender association, be cherished by many and this must be sympathetically allowed for. The hymn is, after all, the people's property. It is to be borne in mind that music in the church is to be a help to the worshipper and his susceptibilities should be considered. Musical education has much ground to cover before the best forms come to be popular ".

His choirs reflected the qualities that characterised his organ work. Purity of tone, unerring attack, instinctive taste, rhythmic balance—all were there. He demanded of men and boys alike the same high standard he set himself and though he never seemed to work them hard his choirs were always among the finest in the country. He never forgot that the choir constitute the chief medium for the musical part of the service, nor did he allow them to forget it either.

That sense of service in the worship of God gave a unity to all his work as a church musician. His instinctive knowledge of what was needed gave him a sureness of touch which bred its own confidence. One of his daughters told him towards the end of his life that she thought his playing of the hymns in Salisbury Cathedral was on the slow side. He replied : " Yes, your mother thinks so too. But I know what is fitting ". *Fitting.* It was the leit-motif of his work for the Church and he was constantly urging the responsibility that devolved on organists for adjusting their contributions to the conditions prevailing.

His conception of the dignity and reverence needed in an organist dates back to an earlier and less self-conscious age. The man whose ideals were formed in the organ loft of St. Paul's Cathedral in the spacious days of Victoria was not likely to lower his standards in the hope of popularising his appeal. To him the Cathedral service was an ideal " to be listened to with reverence and with a mind open to its message delivered through liturgy and service and anthem, the contribution of men of genius through the centuries. The trained choir of a cathedral should be allowed to create an atmosphere and not be subject to the irresponsible contribution of any person unable to resist a self-satisfied desire to join in, irrespective of a voice or the ability to use it properly. After all, it is no disgrace to be unmusical, but humility is desirable ".

He felt that a strongly marked line should be drawn between churches and cathedrals in this matter and considered it unfortunate that while so many churches aimed at imitating the cathedral service, often well beyond their scope, a great effort was on foot to congregationalise the cathedral service.

Throughout his work as a church musician there was an alert intelligence, a logic, that cut through the loose thinking and sentiment which are apt to cloak so much religious observance. Only one quality, in his eyes, was good enough for the worship of the church—the best.

" Thou shalt love the Lord thy God . . . with all thy mind ", he would quote. And again :

" Sing ye praises with understanding ".

VII

NO genius can be free from egotism. The sense of greatness within them impels them to demand notice from the world. Alcock was very much an artist in that his own concerns were to him of paramount importance and indeed the specialised nature of his work tended to intensify this. He loved to talk of his feelings and experiences but he was so interested himself and could make such a good story out of anything that his hearers were generally as engrossed in his affairs as he was.

He was at all times at the mercy of his artistic temperament. Moods of black depression would descend on him that he could make no effort to throw off. They often had no ostensible cause, though he was highly susceptible to weather and lack of sun or prolonged wind drove him to extremes of irritability. In middle life he must often have been difficult to live with for he was over-driven with work and money troubles and a growing family in a small house must have been a constant strain

Photo by] [Hughes, London

Sir Walter Alcock in the year he was Knighted

Choir Practice
at Salisbury.

Walter and Naomi in 1945.

Showing his Engines to the Salisbury Choristers.
Photo by permission of the Keystone Press Associated.

Fishing—

"*He took infinite pains over whatever might be occupying him.*"

on his delicately balanced nerves. But he often laughed at himself for his testiness and would tell a story of how in the train from Surbiton to Waterloo one day he found himself in a carriage with a man who cleared his throat at minute intervals in such a maddening way that Alcock changed carriages at Wimbledon, only to find himself opposite to a man whose face had a nervous twitch that it was impossible not to watch !

This faculty for laughing at himself was very endearing. " How green I was ", he would say and tell of how, asked as a very young man to contribute to a series of recitals at the Albert Hall, he was informed that the fee would be two guineas.

" I sent it at once ", he said, " I thought it was very little to pay for such an honour ".

And he was a complete joy to the Masters' Common Room at Rossall, where he deputised one term for his friend Sweeting. He fell into one trap after another in that experienced company and the delight with which he recollected it all was a tribute alike to their good nature and his.

It would probably surprise his many admirers to be told that he considered himself a weak character. He was very conscious of being at the mercy of his moods and his nerves and he often felt that he was lazy. No one could ever accuse him of shirking any duty that was demanded of him by his work. Only once in his long life was he late for a service and the picture of him this book attempts, affords some idea of his achievements and what they involved in the way of strenuous effort. But he was conscious of the fact that he did not readily seek for work. Walford Davies constantly urged him to compose more and it is a fact that what he did compose was in the highest traditions of its class. But he could not voluntarily apply himself to composition. The lure of the road or of his model engine or of a deck chair in the shade of his Salisbury garden was too strong, the urge to express himself not strong enough. But when asked to write specifically he did so effortlessly and with enjoyment. His Manual on the Organ, written at the request of Messrs. Novello in 1913 is still the standard work on the teaching of the organ and the pieces he included in it for illustration and practice are felicitous as well as being perfectly suited to their purpose. For some reason he always found it an incentive to write for special occasions and when, for instance, he was asked to compose the music for the Sanctus to be sung at the coronation of George V he jotted down the substance of the composition on the back of an envelope as he travelled from Waterloo to Surbiton. And such was the inspiration that when it was sung at the final rehearsal there was spontaneous applause at its conclusion from the performers and the enthusiasm was such that Sir Frederick Bridge let them sing it again. On another occasion he had written an Introduction and Passacaglia for the Three Choirs' Festival of 1933. When he heard Mr. Sumsion's Ostinato, Alcock realised that his own Introduction would be ineffective. So on the morning of the day on which he was to play it he wrote an entirely new one and played it at the conclusion of Evensong as arranged. It is plain, that, given the impetus to begin he wrote easily, with exhilaration and excitement.

How kind he was. In the hundreds of letters that his wife received on his death there were constant references to what he had done for this writer or that. His finely trained sense of quality always enabled him to recognise talent when he saw it and many were the aspiring musicians who received encouragement and practical help from him.

Sir Malcolm Sargent still talks with gratitude of the recognition Alcock gave him when he was unknown and unimportant at Stamford. And after the younger man had become the famous musician Alcock had always known he must the older was not too proud to ask Sargent's advice on the conducting of " The Dream of Gerontius " and was unaffectedly touched and honoured to be lent the famous conductor's own score for the performance in Salisbury Cathedral. Amateur enthusiasts of the organ could be sure of a courteous reception in the organ loft and remembered their visit, not only for the magnificent instrument they were shown so expertly, but for the charming friendliness of the way it was done. He was a delightful companion ; his quick reaction to all happenings, great and small, was a constant stimulus and he had a sense of fun which invested the most ordinary happenings with laughter. He convulsed a rather stately tea-party one day by suddenly describing with a faultless cockney accept a conversation he had overheard between two girls in the street. And at a party given by one of the Bishops of Salisbury which was hanging fire his host asked him if he would play the piano to enliven things. He said he wouldn't play but would be delighted to recite and he broke the ice completely and permanently by his rendering of a long piece of nonsense beginning : " I was sailing my boat over the Alps at midnight one sunny morning ".   The effect must have been electrical.

He was the least complex of men. His standards of conduct were those of an earlier, simpler day. His deep admiration for Charles Dickens as a man and as a writer was definitely clouded when he learnt of the irregularities of his life and he was unaffectedly shocked at much that many take for granted in these modern days. Much of it surprised him when he learnt of it and he never cared to discuss it. A man whose interests were as closely centred in his home and work as his were is safer the most from the world's restlessness. And great though his musical genius was it had not the monopoly of his energies. He still found time for other things. The enthusiasm and intelligence which took him to the top of his profession found their full outlet in his recreations.

His hobbies were many and his pursuit of them was marked by that spirit of enquiry which at its fullest is the mark of the true scientist. Astronomy, photography, electricity and above all engineering, fascinated and absorbed him and he took infinite pains over whatever might be occupying him, toiling patiently for perfection. Though the simplest details of astronomy, as far as mathematics were concerned, were far beyond his grasp, he did not allow that to prevent him dwelling on the mysteries of space and time and finding stars and planets with the aid of his $3\frac{1}{2}$ in. equatorial telescope. It would be set up in the garden and he would gather his family and any available friends to share with him the enchantment of viewing the rings of Saturn, or Jupiter majestic among his moons. He was always astonished at the lack of knowledge, even of interest in this, to him, sublime subject and he possessed most of the works of Proctor, Ball, Flammarion and Sir James Jeans.

He was an enthusiastic and extremely skilful photographer. He spared no pains to get the best possible result and he produced an enormous quantity of beautiful pictures of the places he visited throughout the years that for technical excellence and sense of composition will bear comparison in any company. He possessed a stereiscopic camera with which he obtained hundreds of photographs and he always did his own developing and printing with meticulous care. He had a " magic lantern " for which he made large numbers of slides from photographs he had taken.

All his life machines had an absorbing fascination for him. The engine he contrived so laboriously as a boy was the forerunner of others, more elaborate and still in existence. In 1894 he began building a one-inch scale model of a Midland express engine. He had no drawings. He obtained the chief dimensions by taking measurements with his walking stick at St. Pancras Station and picked up information from the drivers. Later on he constructed a Great Northern eight-foot single to the same scale and both these engines, powered by steam and coal and making, as he would say, all the real smells, would draw a man along the track constructed for the purpose in the back garden.

This mechanical gift served him well in his profession. No organist can have had a better knowledge of the construction of an organ. He habitually, to within a few months of his death, tuned the reeds of the Salisbury organ as they required it and on more than one occasion was able to put right some mechanical defect that happened to develop in some organ that he was playing. He took a personal and intelligent interest in the restoration of the Salisbury organ, the funds for which he was largely responsible for collecting and his expert knowledge of the quality of the original voicing made him insist that it should not be touched. This special knowledge of his made him much in demand as a consultant on organs and it is probably true to say that his advice was sought in building or repairing the majority of the more important instruments since the beginning of the century.

His love of the road, which his early cycling days implanted in him, together with this knack for engines made motoring a real joy to him. The cars which he in turn possessed and which were all that he could afford were mostly in an advanced stage of decay and the task of reviving and transforming them brought its own reward. He loved them all as creatures of his own hands and never tired of wondering at their performance, turning frequently to whoever might be sitting beside him to draw attention to some hill achieved in top gear or to the smooth running produced by yet another ingenious adjustment to the inner parts. It was a love which only occasionally received a jolt when he found himself in the sleek, powerful cars affected by his sons-in-law. Then he would say wistfully :

" Of course, I realise I don't know what modern motoring is ".

But back at the wheel of his own car he recaptured all the old delight. As he once wrote :

"The majority of motorists in these days can have little idea of what we old-timers endured and, I may say, enjoyed. Roadside motoring as we called it is now nothing more serious than a change of wheel or some trifling readjustment. With us it usually involved a major operation. I once felt sure that I could improve the running of an old tri-car I had by reducing the travel of the inlet valve. So I turned up a brass washer in the lathe and fitted it in time for a journey up the Great North Road. All went well until I reached an out-of-the-way place, when " something took place " in the engine. On investigation I found that my brass washer had disintegrated in the heat. I removed the dome and saw some pieces of brass still on the piston. To have removed the cylinder would have meant losing the water and there was no supply at hand. But I had some sandwiches with me which contained butter. With a small stick anointed with butter I called for and collected the pieces of brass and completed the journey without mishap.

"We had in those days to carry a book containing the addresses of those who sold petrol. The fuel cost 8d. a gallon and its quality was that of aviation petrol. There was no taxation. There were neither number plates nor windscreens ".

From those days onward he scoured the country on a series of old crocks, graduating eventually to a comparatively modern Morris Oxford and thence to a 1937 Austin Ten which he viewed with as much excitement and pride as he did his first pennyfarthing bicycle. Among these vehicles was an Autobyk which he acquired during the war at the age of eighty. On this he would go fishing, a pastime he had enjoyed in his youth when he used to catch roach and perch in the Kennet and on Lady Freake's water at Fulwell Park, but now on the trout streams around Salisbury he learnt to throw a fly and was given many hours' of happiness and peace by the generosity of his friends who made him free of their rivers.

On this Autobyk in 1942, indomitable as ever, he made the journey from Salisbury to his daughter's house in Rutland—a distance of 140 miles. He started at 10 a.m. and arrived at 5 p.m., looking forward to his tea. The freedom of the road was still his.

When, a few weeks before his death, knowing as he must have done that he had ridden his last mile, he was bidding goodbye to this same daughter as she left him to drive back to Rutland.

I shall think of you at six o'clock ", he said. " You will be at Kettering. You will be just turning the wheel to the left and slackening your foot on the accelerator as you turn into the road to Uppingham ".

They were the last words she ever heard him say.

His was a happy life. He never had much money but he managed to do most of the things he wanted to do. He had little business sense and very little idea of commercialising his gifts. If he had stayed in London he might have prospered more greatly in the material sense, but it would have been at the expense of his spirit.

He wanted to be organist of Salisbury Cathedral and he achieved his ambition.

www.ingramcontent.com/pod-product-compliance
Lightning Source LLC
LaVergne TN
LVHW051505090426
835512LV00010B/2352